Venus

Earth

Asteroid Belt

Saturn

Neptune

A Look at
Neptune

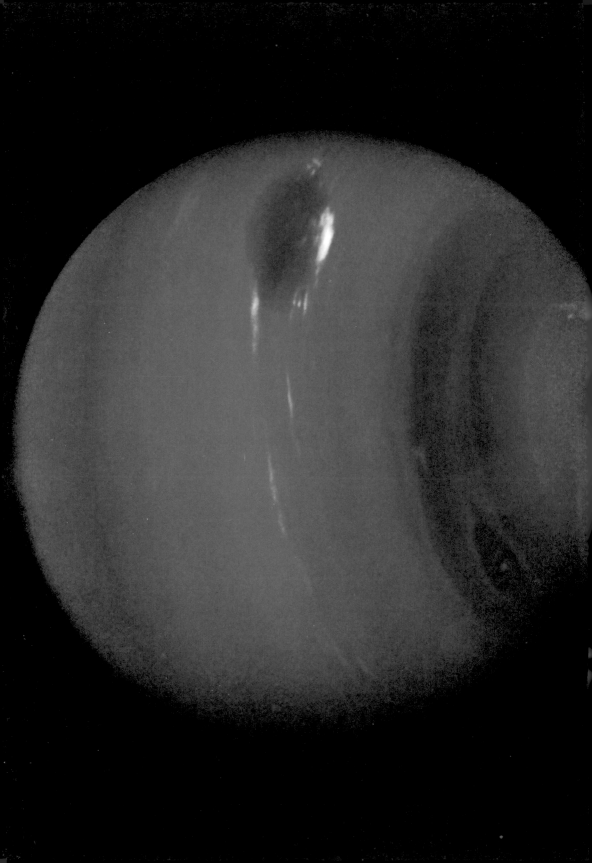

A Look at

Neptune

John Tabak

Franklin Watts

A DIVISION OF SCHOLASTIC INC.
NEW YORK · TORONTO · LONDON · AUCKLAND
SYDNEY · MEXICO CITY · NEW DELHI · HONG KONG
DANBURY, CONNECTICUT

FOR LEO

Photographs © 2003: California Institute of Technology: 21, 24; Corbis Images: 37, 101 (Roger Ressmeyer), cover, 14, 26, 30, 82; Hulton|Archive/Getty Images: 28; Mary Evans Picture Library: 20; NASA: 70 (ESA/STSI), 73 (H. Hammel/Massachusetts Institute of Technology), 2, 8, 11, 12, 13, 32, 44, 45, 56, 62, 64, 65, 66, 67, 93, 97, 98, 102; North Wind Picture Archives: 22; Olivier Staiger: 40, 88; Photo Researchers, NY: 46, 106 (Julian Baum/SPL), 55 (Lynette Cook/SPL), 78 (Simon Fraser/SPL), 80 (David Parker/SPL), 49 (Seth Shostak/SPL); Photri Inc.: 17, 43, 52, 60; W.M. Keck Observatory/AO Staff/LLNL: 81.

The photograph on the cover shows a false color composite photograph of Neptune, produced from images taken by *Voyager 2* in 1989. The photograph across from the title page shows an image of Neptune taken by *Voyager 2* in 1989.

Library of Congress Cataloging-in-Publication Data
   Tabak, John.
   A look at Neptune / by John Tabak.
      p. cm. – (Out of this world)
Summary: Describes the discovery and observation of the planet Neptune and what has been learned about it, particularly from the Voyager spacecraft mission.
Includes bibliographical references and index.
      ISBN 0-531-12267-0 (lib. bdg.) 0-531-15584-6 (pbk.)
      1. Neptune (Planet)—Juvenile literature. [1. Neptune (Planet).]   I. Title.
II. Out of this world (Franklin Watts, Inc.)
QB691.T33   2003   523.48'1—dc21
                                                              2002002023

2 3 4 5 6 7 8 9 10 R 12 11 10 09 08 07 06 05 04

Contents

A Look at Neptune

Voyager 2 took this false-color image of Neptune. Objects deep in Neptune's atmosphere appear as blue, while those at higher altitudes appear closer to white. The white flash near the bottom of Neptune is a high-altitude cloud above the planet's Great Dark Spot.

So Far Away

Neptune, the third most massive planet in our solar system, is almost unimaginably far away. It's about thirty times farther from the Sun than Earth is. Saturn, the sixth most distant planet from the Sun, is about one-third of the distance from the Sun to Neptune. Even Uranus, the seventh planet in the solar system, is only two-thirds of the way to Neptune. (The greater their distance from the Sun, the more spread out the planets are.) A rocket traveling at one million miles per hour (1.6 million kilometers per hour) would need more than one hundred days to go from Earth to Neptune. A rocket that traveled at the top speed of the *Apollo* rocket, the fastest rocket ever to take humans into space, would require well over a decade to travel from Earth to Neptune.

Because Neptune is so far from the Sun, it's forever in the dark. As light travels outward from the Sun, it spreads out. The more it spreads out, the fainter it becomes. By the time sunlight has traveled as far as Neptune, the Sun's light is very weak and very, very dim. The Sun is about nine hundred times brighter when viewed from Earth than it is when viewed from Neptune. When viewed from Neptune, the Sun looks like a solitary, faraway streetlight shining though a cold, clear, moonless night. It doesn't look like the big, bright, hot star that we experience on a cloudless summer day.

Scientists have always had a difficult time learning about Neptune. It's too far away to see clearly. In fact, two hundred years ago no one knew that this dark, windy world existed. Since its discovery in 1846, scientists have used a variety of clever ideas and technologies to learn about Neptune:

- Scientists calculated the mass of Neptune. This means they have calculated how much material makes up Neptune.

- Scientists know the chemical composition of Neptune's atmosphere.

- Scientists know a little bit about the weather on Neptune.

- Scientists discovered eight moons in orbit about Neptune.

- Scientists recorded the atmospheric pressure on Triton, Neptune's largest moon.

Scientists learned all of this and more just by looking. No sample of Neptune's atmosphere has ever been brought back to Earth for analysis. No one has ever placed a barometer on any of Neptune's moons to measure the atmospheric pressure. No space probe has ever dived beneath the cloud tops to see what lies beneath. To learn about Neptune, scientists depend on light, logic, and imagination.

There was one brief visit by one very famous spacecraft in 1989. That was *Voyager 2*. *Voyager* hurtled past Neptune at a top speed of more than 37,000 mph (59,000 kph). It made as many measurements as possible, and it took as many pictures as possible, but there wasn't much time to do either. The *Voyager* mission to Neptune was a success. It was, in fact, a huge breakthrough, but it left most questions unanswered.

This is a full-scale model of the *Voyager 2* spacecraft. Launched August 20, 1977, *Voyager 2* made studies of Jupiter, Saturn, Uranus, and Neptune.

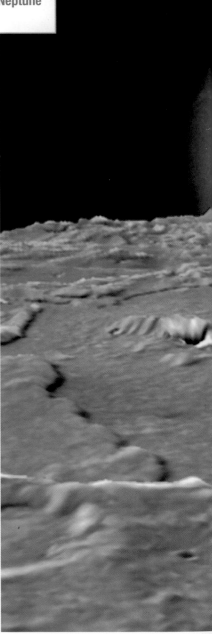

Created by *Voyager 2*, this composite view shows Neptune rising over Triton's horizon. To a viewer on Triton, Neptune would appear to move laterally along the horizon.

Since *Voyager's* flyby, scientists have continued to learn about Neptune. Like their predecessors, modern scientists continue to rely on analyses of the sunlight that Neptune reflects back toward Earth. In fact, telescopes (and the various pieces of equipment attached to the scopes), mathematics, computer simulations, and *Voyager's* data are the only tools scientists will have to explore Neptune for the indefinite future. Despite this, scientists never stopped learning about Neptune. In fact, scientists were busy learning about this planet even *before* it was discovered.

In this book we will learn how scientists found Neptune and what they know today. We will even learn a little about how scientists have learned about this faraway world. Imagination is the key. It takes imagination as well as science and mathematics to learn about Neptune. Not just because Neptune is dark and far away, but because it is a world that is completely unlike our own.

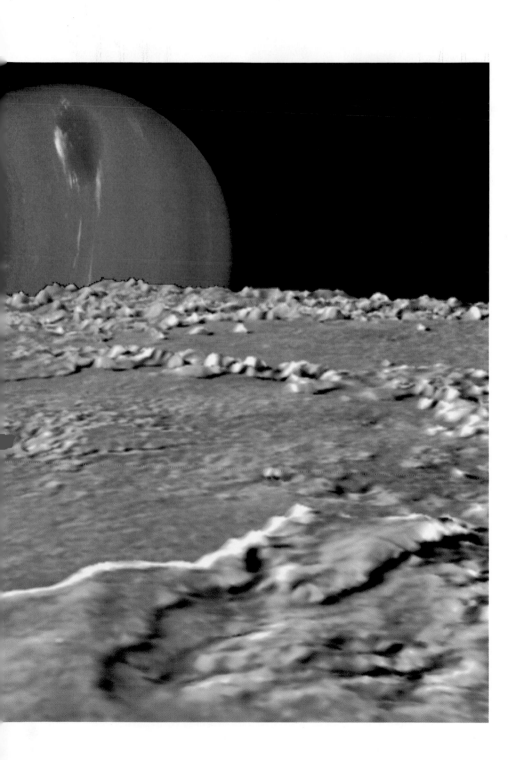

An orrery is a device that showed the positions and motions of the bodies in the solar system. It was invented by James Ferguson, an 18th-century Scottish inventor and astronomer.

Chapter 1

The Discovery of Neptune

Neptune was discovered in 1846. The discovery of Neptune was one of the great scientific accomplishments of the nineteenth century. It wasn't discovered by an astronomer sitting at a telescope; it was discovered by two astronomers sitting at their desks. That the position of a never-before-seen planet could be deduced with the help of some clever mathematics surprised many scientists and nonscientists alike. Neptune's discovery showed people in all walks of life that, after centuries of hard work, scientists were finally developing a deep understanding of the laws of nature. Using a lot of science, math, and imagination, two scientists, working independently, calculated the location of a new, previously unidentified planet. That planet was Neptune. To understand how they went about this discovery, we need to take a look at how and why planets move the way they do.

Kepler's Laws of Planetary Motion

The German astronomer and mathematician Johannes Kepler is the author of *Kepler's laws of planetary motion*. These "laws" describe *how* planets move about the Sun. His laws describe the overall shape of the solar system and how the speed of each planet changes as it moves along its orbit. These were difficult discoveries to make. One reason for the difficulty is that Kepler studied the motions of the planets without any real understanding of *why* planets move along the paths that they do. He was missing this important piece of the puzzle because the *law of gravity* hadn't been discovered yet. (The law of gravity is the physical principle that explains how gravity works. We'll learn more about this law later.) Kepler died more than fifty years before the law of gravity was discovered. Kepler's work was further hindered by the fact that the kind of mathematics that would have made his work easier hadn't been developed yet.

What Kepler did have were measurements of the positions of the planets in the night sky. Nowadays, we call this type of information raw data. Kepler didn't know many mathematical techniques for analyzing these raw data. This wasn't his fault. The techniques hadn't been invented yet. Instead, he pondered the data for years. Gradually, he developed a very accurate understanding of how planets move about the Sun. It was a great scientific triumph that was then used in the discovery and exploration of Neptune.

The First Law

Planets orbit the Sun along elliptical paths. The Sun is located at one focus of the *ellipse*. Ellipses look like slightly flattened circles.

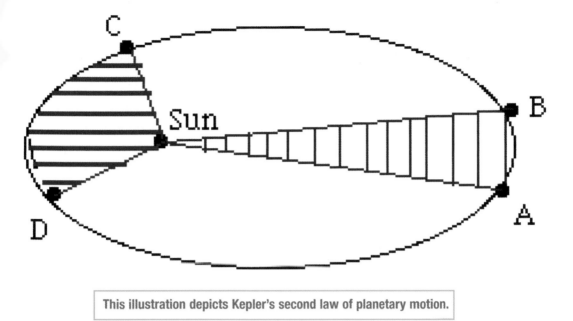

This illustration depicts Kepler's second law of planetary motion.

The Second Law

The speed of each planet changes as it orbits the Sun. A planet moves faster when it's closer to the Sun and slower when it's farther away. Kepler also noticed something very special about *how* the speed changes. If you were to plot a planet's orbital path on a piece of paper and connect the position of the planet with the position of the Sun, the line connecting the planet's position with the Sun's position would "sweep out" an area shaped like a slice of pie as the planet moved along its orbit. The further along its orbit the planet moved, the bigger the slice it would sweep out. What Kepler discovered is that each planet's speed changes in such a way that it sweeps out equal areas in equal times.

The Third Law

Kepler's third law relates the distance of a planet from the Sun with the time it takes to complete one orbit. Kepler discovered that every planet obeys this special relationship. Here's the relationship: Let the letter D represent the planet's average distance from the Sun, and let the letter T represent the length of time necessary for the planet to complete one orbit about the Sun. The distance D and the time T differ from planet to planet, but for each planet $D^3 = T^2$. (Here D^3, or D cubed, means

	D Average Distance from Sun (in AUs)	T Period of Rotation (in Earth years)	D^3	T^2
MERCURY	0.39	0.24	0.06	0.06
VENUS	0.72	0.62	0.37	0.38
EARTH	1	1	1	1
MARS	1.52	1.88	3.51	3.53
JUPITER	5.20	11.86	141	141
SATURN	9.54	29.46	868	868
URANUS*	19.201	83.759	7,079	70,156
NEPTUNE*	30.047	164.79	27,127	27,156
PLUTO*	39.238	248.05	60,412	61,529

*Kepler didn't know about Uranus, Neptune, and Pluto, though you can see that his laws hold for these planets as well. Notice, too, that for some of the planets D^3 and T^2 are very close but not quite equal. The important point for now is to recognize that while it might not be exact—few mathematical models are—the situation is very close to being as Kepler described.

$D \times D \times D$, and T^2, which is T squared, means $T \times T$.) By the way, we've expressed the average distance from the Sun to each planet in astronomical units, or AUs. One astronomical unit is defined as the distance from Earth to the Sun. Two AUs is twice as far.

Kepler's first two laws helped these early astronomers understand how planets move about the Sun.

The third law allows them to do something amazing. Once scientists determined T, the time it takes the planet to complete one orbit about the Sun, *they could compute D,* the distance of the planet from the Sun measured in astronomical units. This is important because T could be measured from Earth by watching how quickly the planet moved against the background stars. So they measured T and then (with the help of Kepler's third law) they computed D by solving the equation $D^3 = T^2$. This involves only a little algebra. It's the kind of algebra you may already have done in your math class. (And if you haven't done this kind of problem yet, you will soon.) Once the astronomers identified the distance from the Sun to Earth in kilometers, they could also compute the average distance of every planet from the Sun in kilometers. They multiplied each planet's distance from the Sun measured in AUs by the Earth/Sun distance measured in kilometers.

Kepler's third law is what enabled astronomers to estimate Uranus's distance from the Sun when it was discovered in the eighteenth century as well as Neptune's distance from the Sun when it was discovered in the nineteenth century. This was a wonderful accomplishment. Remember that they obtained their data by looking through their telescopes and when they looked through their telescopes at these planets, all they saw were small, blurry dots.

Johannes Kepler

Johannes Kepler (1571-1630) was the first person in history with a detailed understanding of how planets orbit the Sun. During Kepler's life, there were several competing theories about the geometry of the solar system. Some thought that the Sun and planets orbit Earth. Others thought that some planets orbit the Sun and that the Sun orbits Earth. Early in his adult life Kepler concluded that all planets, including Earth, orbit the Sun.

Even as a young man Kepler worked hard to try to understand the shape of the solar system, but his big break came when he was hired as an assistant to the great Danish astronomer Tycho Brahe (1546-1601). Brahe's observatory had no telescopes. They hadn't been invented yet. Instead, the astronomers measured the positions of planets and stars in the night sky with instruments that looked like protractors and surveyor's

The Discovery of Uranus

The discovery of Neptune begins in 1781 with the discovery of Uranus, the seventh planet in the solar system. The German-born British astronomer and musician William Herschel was carefully scanning the night sky with his telescope when he saw a previously unknown object. Because Herschel was an experienced and transits (but without the lenses). Such instruments may seem crude to us, but in the hands of these scientists, these instruments produced measurements that were far more exact than any previous ones. The measurements were entered into tables and when Brahe died, Kepler got the tables. He analyzed them again and again. Over the course of many years, he developed a mathematical model that accounted for these measurements. This model is called Kepler's three laws of planetary motion.

Kepler worked hard to communicate his ideas, and he exercised great creativity in his attempts to convey his views. In addition to his scientific arguments, he also compared the motion of the planets through space with music. Each planet could be imagined as playing its part in a musical composition, he said. Each planet's motion contributed to a harmonious whole. The phrase "the music of the spheres" is Kepler's. Four hundred years later, you can still hear that phrase on science shows and see it in science books (like this one) about the solar system.

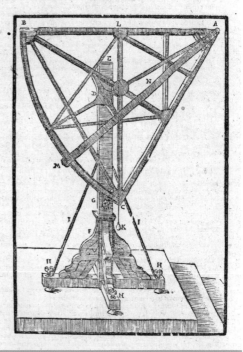

SEXTANS ASTRONOMICVS, PROUT ALTITUDINIBUS inferuit.

Before the invention of the telescope, instruments like this sextant were used to make astronomical measurements.

careful observer he knew it wasn't a star. Eventually, he recognized it as an undiscovered planet. (Other astronomers had already observed Uranus, but they hadn't recognized it as a planet.) The discovery made Herschel famous. But Uranus's discovery wasn't based on any deep scientific insights. The discovery of Uranus was an accident.

William Herschel looks through the telescope
that he and his sister, Caroline, built.

That Uranus existed at all came as a shock to people. For thousands of years everyone had known about Mercury, Venus, Mars, Jupiter, and Saturn. The idea that there were worlds beyond Saturn was a new and exciting one. People wanted to find out as much as they could about this distant new planet. Astronomers immediately began to measure Uranus's position in the night sky. They did this so that they could determine its orbit. They wanted to know its precise orbit so that they could predict its future position. (Predicting a planet's motions is one important way of understanding a planet. It not only tells how long the planet's year is; it can, when used with Kepler's third law, tell us the planet's distance from the Sun.) Determining Uranus's path through the night sky required many careful measurements.

In the years following the discovery of Uranus, astronomers used Kepler's laws to interpret their measurements. Kepler's laws were powerful tools that they used in their attempt to predict Uranus's future positions in the night sky, but Kepler's laws weren't their only tools. Kepler's ideas were still very influential, but these astronomers had also gone beyond Kepler. Remember that Kepler died more than 150 years before the discovery of Uranus. During that time, science had progressed. These astronomers didn't just understand *how* planets move; they understood *why*: planets move through space the way that they do because of the force of gravity.

These astronomers knew one more thing that Johannes Kepler did not know—and this is very important to our story—they knew that Kepler's laws aren't 100 percent accurate. Planets don't quite travel along perfect ellipses, which is what Kepler thought. Planetary speeds don't vary quite as Kepler had described. Years of careful measurements of the motions of all the known planets showed these astronomers that orbital ellipses are *almost* perfect and planetary speeds vary *almost*—but not quite—as Kepler said they did. These astronomers knew that each planet exhibited small deviations in its orbital motion. They called these deviations *perturbations* and even two hundred years ago they knew what caused the perturbations that they measured.

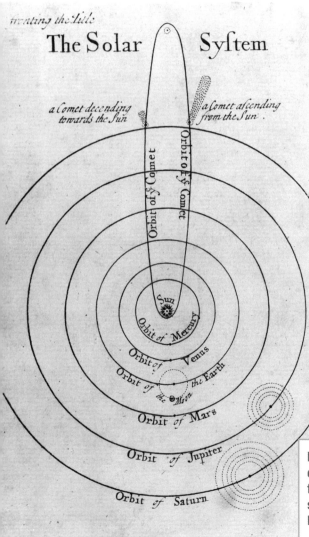

Planets (for the most part) move along the paths that Kepler predicted because they move under the gravitational force exerted by the Sun. But other objects besides the Sun have gravity. Planets have gravity, and one planet's gravity can be strong enough to affect the motion of its neighbors in space. Compared to the Sun, however, every planet's gravity is very weak. That means that the effect caused by one planet's gravity on the orbit of its neighbor is small when compared to the effect of the Sun. These small effects were the perturbations that scientists had learned to measure.

Even without the use of telescopes, early astronomers were able to make fairly accurate measurements of the solar system, with the help of theories such as Kepler's laws of planetary motion.

But they didn't just measure perturbations. As their knowledge of the solar system and of the law of gravity improved, astronomers learned to predict with great precision the orbital motions of the planets. By 1840 they had even learned to predict the perturbations in the orbital motion of each planet. They could do all of this with every known planet *except Uranus.*

After decades of measuring the position of Uranus and then using those measurements to predict Uranus's future positions, they found that they could not explain or predict the perturbations that they observed in Uranus's orbit. Uranus didn't go quite where they expected it to go. This was surprising and frustrating because Uranus's motion indicated a gap in their knowledge of the solar system. Something was missing. Because they were sure of their measurements, they concluded that the problem was in their predictions. And remember that the problem was only with Uranus. They could, for example, accurately predict the paths that Jupiter and Saturn traveled across the night sky. So the obvious question was: why couldn't they also predict the motion of Uranus?

Astronomers began to suspect the existence of an eighth planet, located even further from the Sun than Uranus. They began to suspect that the gravitational tug of this unseen planet caused the additional perturbations in Uranus's orbit that they clearly observed but could not otherwise explain.

Revealed!

In the 1840s, sixty years after the discovery of Uranus, two astronomers, working independently of each other, John Couch Adams and Urbain Jean Joseph Le Verrier, decided to try to locate the

Gravity is the glue that holds the universe together. It's the force that causes planets to orbit the Sun. It causes apples to fall from trees and the stars themselves to orbit the center of the galaxy to which they belong. The first person to accurately describe the force of gravity was the mathematician and scientist Isaac Newton (1642–1727). His description is called the law of gravity.

Newton was very interested in how all types of forces affect the motions of all types of objects. Prior to his work on gravity, Newton had already discovered that any change in any object's motion depends solely on the forces that act on the object. That's why it was so important to accurately describe how the force of gravity works: understanding the force of gravity was the key to understanding the motions of the planets about the Sun. What he discovered is that the strength of the gravitational pull between two bodies is proportional to the product of the masses of the two bodies divided by the square of the distance between them. In symbols it looks like this:

$$F = Gm_1 m_2 / d^2$$

The letter F stands for the force of gravity. The symbol m_1 is the mass of one body and m_2 is the mass of the other. The letter d represents the distance between the two bodies. G, called the gravitational constant, is the constant of proportionality, which is just another way of saying that G is the same for any two masses at any two distances. So we need only measure G once to know it for every situation, and by 1846, the year of Neptune's discovery, G had already been measured.

One thing that the law of gravity tells us is that a really big mass exerts a really big gravitational pull. This explains why the Sun exerts the greatest gravitational pull of any object in the solar system. The Sun's mass is huge compared to the mass of any planet. In fact, the Sun's mass is huge when compared to the mass of all the planets combined. It contains more than 99 percent of the mass of the entire solar system. The law of gravity also tells us that the gravitational force that two bodies exert on each other weakens the farther apart the bodies move. That's because the larger d becomes the smaller the quotient $Gm_1 m_2 / d^2$ becomes. The formula $F = Gm_1 m_2 / d^2$ is one of the most famous discoveries in the history of science.

Isaac Newton

suspected eighth planet. They didn't look through a telescope, though. The night sky is a big place and they didn't know where to look. And don't forget: even if astronomers know the location of a planet, that doesn't mean that they can see it. The planet they're searching for may be below the horizon. It may be located on the other side of the Sun from Earth. This is true for all planets. Each year each planet is visible for part of the year in Earth's night sky, but for part of the year each planet is invisible. It's lost in the glare of the Sun. Looking for an object in the night sky when you have no idea where it is, or even if it's in the night sky at all, is just too difficult and time-consuming a task.

Le Verrier and Adams had a different approach. At the time it was a radical idea. No astronomer had ever tried to solve this kind of problem before. Their approach to finding the mystery planet—assuming that the planet existed at all—was to analyze the perturbations in Uranus's orbit and then to deduce the location of the mystery planet. This was a purely mathematical approach, and it is a very difficult mathematical problem to solve. It's one thing to predict the perturbation caused by one planet in the orbit of another when you know the locations and masses of both planets. It's a much harder problem to predict the existence and location of one planet when all you have are measurements of another planet's orbit. Many astronomers of the time considered this an impossible task. Nevertheless, John Couch Adams in Britain and Urbain Jean Joseph Le Verrier in France decided to try to find a whole new world by analyzing the unexplained perturbations in the orbit of Uranus.

The first of these two astronomers to begin was Adams. A prominent British astronomer, George Biddell Airy, a man far better known than Adams at the time, said, "I give it as my opinion, without hesita-

Besides his work that led to the discovery of Neptune, John Couch Adams is also known for his discovery that the orbit of the Leonid meteor shower was very similar to that of a comet.

tion, that we are not yet in such a state as to give the smallest hope of making out the nature of any external action on the planet." In other words, in his opinion, Adams didn't stand a chance.

Unfortunately for Adams, Airy was in charge of the Royal Observatory at Greenwich, and later, when Adams had finished his work, he would need the help of the staff at the observatory to confirm his prediction. But Airy's skepticism didn't discourage Adams. He solved the problem. It took him five years of hard work but he finally computed the position of the new planet in the night sky. He knew where to look to find Neptune.

Le Verrier began later than Adams. He spent two years of his life working on the problem. He solved it, too. He finished a little behind Adams, but Le Verrier and Adams arrived at essentially the same solution. It was Le Verrier, however, who got the credit for being the first to solve the problem.

Very few astronomers believed that what Le Verrier and Adams had attempted was possible. It wasn't just Airy. Many astronomers thought that Adams and Le Verrier were wasting their time. It just seemed like the problem that they were attempting to solve was too difficult. So when Adams claimed to have located the unknown planet he had a hard time convincing the big Greenwich observatory to use its telescope to search the night sky near the position that he had computed. (Airy was still in charge.) The people at the observatory didn't believe Adams could have succeeded. They didn't want to waste their time or their money in a futile search. Unfortunately for Adams, they wouldn't have been wasting their time. Instead, they would have discovered a planet.

Urbain Jean Joseph Le Verrier

Le Verrier, however, was able to locate astronomers at an observatory in Germany who were willing to point their telescope at the position in the sky that he had computed. And when, in 1846, they looked, they found the planet that we now call Neptune at almost the exact spot that Le Verrier had predicted. The whole search took them about an hour. Le Verrier's remarkable prediction was confirmed.

The work of Adams and Le Verrier showed that scientists were beginning to understand nature in a new way, a more profound way. They had, after all, located a planet that no one knew was there. Unlike William Herschel and the discovery of Uranus, Adams and Le Verrier had discovered Neptune without looking through a telescope! They needed a telescope only to confirm their prediction. Adams and Le Verrier found a previously unknown planet using only the disturbances created by the "gravitational wake" that it made as it plowed through the darkness of outer space.

Neptune's moon, Triton

Neptune Before *Voyager*

B etween Neptune's discovery in 1846 and the flyby of the *Voyager* 2 spacecraft in 1989, all astronomers saw when they looked at Neptune through their telescopes was a small, dim, blurry, blue-green disc. Neptune is too dim to be seen with the naked eye. As astronomers and engineers designed and built bigger and better telescopes, our telescopic image of Neptune got bigger but not much better. Neptune's image remained blurry because of the blurring effects of Earth's atmosphere. It appeared as a blue-green smudge on a black background. Prior to *Voyager*'s flyby even the best views of Neptune were unimpressive. Despite this, several important properties of Neptune were discovered during this time. In this chapter, we'll find out what scientists learned about Neptune in the days before *Voyager* and how they learned it.

To understand the difficulties that these astronomers faced in learning about Neptune, it's important to keep in mind that astronomers can't touch, hear, smell, or taste Neptune. No spacecraft has ever returned from Neptune with a sample for analysis. And the telescopic images of Neptune were, for the first 140 years after its discovery, lousy. Blurry images were all that these scientists had to work with. That did not stop them, however. Eventually, they settled on three main approaches to learning about Neptune. The three main approaches that they had all depended upon are as follows:

- Scientists used telescopes to study images of Neptune and its moons.

- Scientists used spectrographs. A spectrograph is a device that astronomers used in conjunction with a telescope to record the light that Neptune reflects back from the Sun toward Earth.

- Scientists used telescopes to study occultations of stars by Neptune. Stellar occultations, or occultations for short, occur when a planetary object, in this case Neptune, passes between a star and Earth. When this happens Neptune blots out the star's light. (As we'll soon see, in the hands of a good astronomer, a great deal can be learned from an occultation.)

We'll see how astronomers learned something important about Neptune using one of the techniques listed above. It's amazing that so much can be learned from such "simple" observations!

Observing Mass

Mass is the amount of material in an object. On Earth, the more mass an object has the more it weighs. In outer space, where everything is weightless, mass must be measured differently.

Neptune's mass was one of the first things scientists "observed" about the planet, which, in a way, is surprising because you can't see mass at all. Mass can't be directly observed for the same reason that you can't observe the weight of a closed box. A box may be light because it's empty, or it may be heavy because it's filled with rocks. We can't tell by looking because empty boxes and full boxes usually look the same.

Suppose, however, that we observe a strong person struggling to lift a box. The person's face might be turning red. His or her muscles may be straining. If we observe these effects, then we can be sure of the cause: the box contains something very massive. We can be sure that the box contains something massive even if we have no idea what's inside the box. This is the idea behind how scientists first estimated Neptune's mass. They observed the effects of Neptune's gravity by looking through their telescopes. The effects of Neptune's gravity enabled them to compute the mass necessary to produce the effects that they observed. Here's how they did it.

Once a planet's mass is determined, the strength of its gravity can be computed. That's a consequence of the law of gravity: the more mass an object has, the stronger its gravitational pull must be.

The opposite is true, too. If we know how strong a planet's gravity is, we can also compute how much mass the planet has. Furthermore, to determine how strong a planet's gravity is, we need only observe how its gravity affects other, nearby objects. That's why the discovery of Triton, Neptune's largest moon, was so important.

Triton, one of the largest moons in the solar system, was discovered in 1846, seventeen days after Neptune was first identified as a planet. Even from a distance of almost 3 billion miles (5 billion km), scientists could observe how long it took Triton to orbit Neptune. It takes almost six days to go around once. Astronomers could also estimate the size of Triton's orbit by measuring the maximum distance separating Triton from Neptune in their telescopic images. Armed with this information and the law of gravity, they were able to compute how much gravitational force Neptune had to apply to Triton to keep it moving along its orbital path. And because knowing the strength of a planet's gravity allows one to find the planet's mass, they were able to estimate Neptune's mass from these simple visual observations. They discovered that Neptune is approximately seventeen times more massive than Earth.

For about 100 years after its discovery, Triton was Neptune's only known moon. Then, in 1949, Neptune's second largest moon, Nereid, was first observed. Nereid is much smaller than Triton. You can tell by the fact that about a century passed between the discovery of Triton and the discovery of Nereid that Nereid is also much harder to observe. Compared to Triton, which as we'll soon see is a very dynamic place, Nereid seems very quiet. In fact, Nereid is just a big rock. Prior to *Voyager*'s arrival at Neptune, Nereid and Triton were the only known moons of Neptune.

Observing Chemistry

The second way that scientists learned about Neptune prior to the arrival of *Voyager 2* was through the use of spectrographs. Spectrographs are used to help astronomers analyze light. Astronomers use

This is the 120-inch Shane Telescope in its dome at the Lick Observatory.

We can see exactly how scientists determined Neptune's mass when the only measurements they could make were visual observations. We can even find Neptune's mass ourselves. By 1846, the year of Neptune's discovery, scientists had learned to apply Kepler's laws, which were originally written to describe the motion of the planets about the Sun, to the motion of moons about the planets. Especially important in this regard was Kepler's third law, which relates the time it takes a planet to complete one orbit to the distance of that planet from the Sun. With the help of the law of gravity, these scientists used Kepler's third law to relate three things: (1) the time it takes for Triton to orbit Neptune, (2) the distance from Triton to Neptune, and (3) the mass of Neptune. In symbols it looks like this:

$$M = \frac{4\pi^2}{G} \longleftrightarrow \frac{D^3}{T^2}$$

- The letter M represents Neptune's mass. (M is measured in kilograms.)

- The letter G is the gravitational constant.

- The letter D represents the average distance of Triton to Neptune. (D is measured in meters.)

- The letter T represents the time it takes Triton to complete one orbit about Neptune. (T is measured in seconds.)

This equation was very useful. When scientists had completed their telescopic observations, they knew every term that appears on the right side of this equation. They could measure D and T by watching Neptune through their telescopes. They had already measured G, the gravitational constant, in the lab, and they knew the number that's represented by the Greek letter π. All they had to do at that point was plug in the numbers on the right side of the equation and do the computations. When they finished, they had a good estimate of Neptune's mass. The current estimate of Neptune's mass is $102{,}440 \times 10^{21}$ kilograms.

You can compute Neptune's mass yourself with the help of a calculator.

- T = 510,000 seconds, which is almost 6 days.

- D = 360,000,000 meters, the distance from the center of Neptune to the center of Triton.

- G = 0.000000000067 m^3/s^2 kg, where m stands for meters, s stands for seconds and kg is the abbreviation for kilogram. (m^3/s^2 kg is often written Nxm^2/kg^2, where N is an abbreviation for the unit of force called a Newton.)

- Your calculator probably has a key for π.

If you calculate Neptune's mass using these numbers, you'll find that your answer is very close to the estimate given above.

spectrographs in conjunction with telescopes to identify which colors the object (in this case Neptune) reflects and which colors it absorbs. This information allows them to identify the chemical composition of a planet by analyzing the sunlight that the planet reflects back toward Earth. Here's how spectrographs work.

Light travels in waves. The *wavelength* of a beam of light is the distance from one peak of the wave to the next. We see light of different wavelengths as different colors. Light that appears blue or violet to us has shorter wavelengths than light that looks red or orange. We can't always rely on our eyes, however, to help us identify the wavelength of a beam of light. Sunlight is the perfect example of how our eyes can sometimes deceive us. Usually we don't see sunlight as different colors even though many different colors are present in the light. When we see sunlight we perceive the mix of colors as ordinary white light, but the colors are still there. We just don't see them. They're lost in the mix.

Rainbows are what we get when we separate out, or unmix, the different colors that are present in sunlight. The colors that appear in a rainbow are the colors that are present in sunlight all the time. As sunlight passes through rain droplets the colors separate and the rainbow appears with the colors arranged according to their wavelength, red at one side of the rainbow, violet at the other.

Spectrographs, like raindrops and prisms, unmix the light. An astronomer uses a telescope to focus a narrow beam of light, which is usually composed of many different wavelengths, through the front end of the spectrograph. (In our case, this is sunlight reflected off Neptune.) The spectrograph spreads out the different wavelengths. It unmixes the light so that the astronomer can analyze the *spectrum*, which is the rainbowlike pattern of colors that forms at the back end of the spectrograph. They do this because they know that each chemical absorbs light at certain wavelengths and reflects the rest of the light. Different chemicals absorb and reflect different wavelengths. The spectrum that the spectrograph shows us is like a rainbow but with certain colors missing. It's the *pattern* of light that the planet absorbs and reflects that the spectrograph reveals. This pattern allows scientists to identify the chemical composition of the body that reflected certain wavelengths of sunlight and absorbed others.

By focusing the sunlight that reflected off Neptune through their spectrographs, astronomers learned that Neptune's atmosphere contains hydrogen, helium, and methane. Methane, by the way, tends to absorb red light and reflect blue light, which is why Neptune looks so blue in pictures.

Detecting Neptune's Rings Without Observing Them

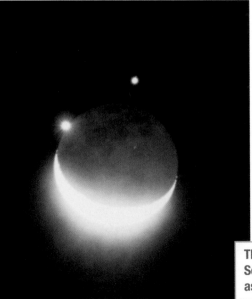

The Dutch scientist Christian Huygens was the first to correctly describe Saturn's huge ring system. That was in 1655. The ring systems that encircle Jupiter, Uranus, and Neptune weren't discovered until much later. In 1977 scientists detected the rings encircling Uranus, and several years later—but prior to *Voyager's* arrival—scientists finally detected

This photo, taken from Ascension Island in the South Atlantic on April 23, 1998, shows the Moon as it passed in front of Venus and Jupiter.

Neptune's rings. They didn't actually see the rings, however. To see the rings they would have to wait until *Voyager*'s arrival at Neptune in 1989. Instead, they detected the effects of the rings on starlight.

When a planet passes between Earth and a star it's called a stellar occultation, or an occultation for short. We say the planet occults the star. During an occultation, the planet blots out the star's light. When a planet *without* rings is observed during an occultation, the observer sees this sequence of events:

- The planet approaches the star.

- The planet blocks out the light of the star as it passes between the star and the observer.

- The planet moves past the star and the star becomes visible again.

It can be a little more complicated when the planet has rings. When rings are present even if the observer can't see the rings themselves, the observer will sometimes see a different sequence of events:

- The planet approaches the star.

- The starlight quickly blinks off and on one or more times. (Each blink lasts for less than a second.)

- The planet moves between the star and the observer, and the starlight is blocked out for a longer period.

- Finally, as the planet moves past the star, the observer sees the star appear to blink on and off one or more times again before it begins to shine steadily from the other side of the planet.

So what's the cause of all that extra blinking? The star appears to blink off momentarily because it's obscured by one of the planet's rings as the ring moves across the observer's field of view. The light blinks back on again as soon as the star clears the other side of the ring. Astronomers have learned to detect the blink even when they can't see the ring.

Beginning early in the 1980s, scientists began to detect starlight quickly blinking on and off during occultations of Neptune. There was something puzzling about these blinks, however. Sometimes during an occultation, scientists would detect a blink on one side of the planet without a corresponding blink on the other. What, they wondered, could cause that kind of phenomenon? Scientists couldn't see any rings, of course. The rings are too far, too thin, and too dim to be visible. Even in the early '80s, however, scientists could observe the effect of the occulting object—whatever it might be!—on starlight. Since they couldn't see the occulting object, they didn't really know what it was. Like Adams and Le Verrier before them, these scientists were trying to decide what kind of object caused the observed effect without ever seeing the object.

Some scientists thought that Neptune's rings might not be rings at all. At first, there was a dispute about whether the blinks were due to an incomplete ring, sometimes called a ring arc, or an undiscovered moon. No one had ever seen a ring arc before, but moons are quite common, so the moon theory had a number of supporters. As additional occultations were observed—and even before *Voyager* reached Neptune—most scientists agreed that the reason for the blinks, isolated or not, had to be some type of ring structure. There were many, however, who thought the asymmetric blinks could best be explained

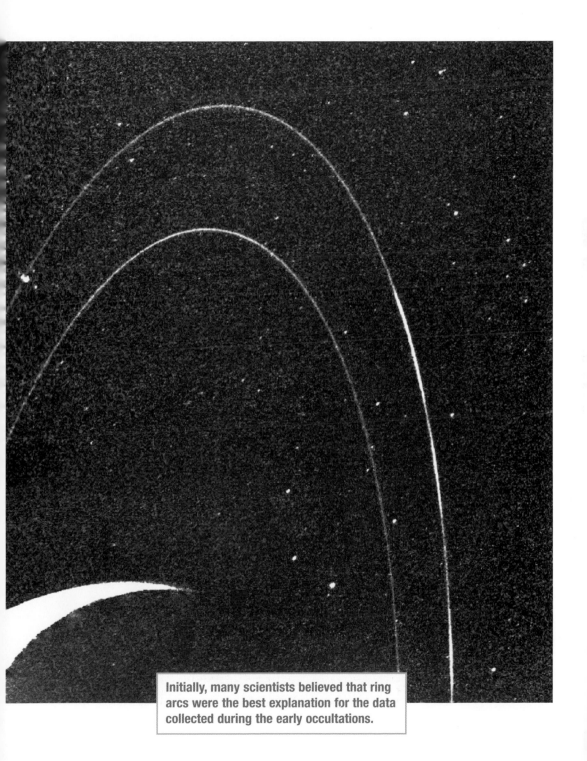

Initially, many scientists believed that ring arcs were the best explanation for the data collected during the early occultations.

Neptune's rings.

by ring arcs. Later, scientists learned that the "arcs" are actually thick clumps in thin rings that completely encircle the planet.

One of the occultations is now thought to have been caused by the occultation of the star by one of Neptune's moons, so the scientists who supported the moon theory weren't entirely wrong.

The three techniques of visual observation, spectrographic analysis, and the observation of stellar occultations continued to play an important role when *Voyager* visited Neptune. They continue, even today, to play an important role in how scientists learn about this faraway planet.

An artist's view of *Voyager 2* approaching Neptune.

Chapter 3

Voyager 2, The Machine

O nly one spacecraft has ever reached Neptune. That was *Voyager 2*. The journey took twelve years. *Voyager 2*'s journey began August 20, 1977, and made its closest approach to Neptune on August 25, 1989.

Voyager 2 doesn't look like the satellites that orbit Earth. Unlike Earth-orbiting satellites, *Voyager* doesn't have any solar panels to convert sunlight into electrical energy. Far past the orbit of Mars, where *Voyager* was designed to work, the Sun's rays are so weak that solar panels couldn't be used. There's not enough sunlight. *Voyager* had to be designed to "live" in the dark.

All the power that runs *Voyager*'s radios, computers, and experiments comes from a nuclear power plant. As nuclear power plants go, however, this one is tiny. It doesn't supply much power. When it comes to using the energy supplied by its nuclear power plant, *Voyager* must be very energy-efficient. The toaster in your kitchen requires far more power to toast bread than *Voyager* required to explore Neptune.

The three computers on *Voyager* weren't the fastest or most powerful computers available in 1977 when *Voyager* was launched. It takes time to build and test the computers on a spacecraft, especially one designed for interplanetary space travel. The circuitry must be carefully protected so that it can withstand the shaking it will receive during launch. It must also be protected from the radiation it will experience in outer space. All of this testing and protecting takes time. So the computers had already been around awhile when *Voyager* was launched. They were already a little old-fashioned. By the time *Voyager* arrived at Neptune twelve years later they were antiques. *Voyager*'s data storage system has a capacity of half a gigabyte. This is a small fraction of the data storage one can get on a modern laptop, but it was still pretty good in 1977.

Voyager was equipped with a variety of scientific instruments as well as two transmitters and multiple antennas. Of special interest to us are Voyager's cameras and *spectrometers*. Spectrometers measure the wavelengths of light waves and (as we'll soon see) certain other types of waves. The cameras were designed to take photographs in dim light. In dim light, a camera must be able to take photographs with long exposure times. That means that the camera must be able to focus on an object for an extended period of time while the dim image is slowly "captured" by the camera. The spectrometers were used to collect additional information about the chemical composition of Neptune's atmosphere, and as we'll soon see, one special spectrometer could also collect information about temperatures.

Artist's impression of *Voyager 2*
during its encounter with Neptune

Nuclear Power on *Voyager*

Voyager is a nuclear-powered spacecraft. At the edge of the solar system, in the dark, in a vacuum, there was no way to get sufficient power to run the spacecraft using 1970's technology except with nuclear energy. (Remember that nothing on *Voyager* was built after 1977, the year of its launch.) All the electrical power necessary to run *Voyager* begins with a small supply of plutonium.

Plutonium is radioactive, which means that the plutonium atoms themselves are unstable. They tend to break apart of their own accord, and each time a plutonium atom breaks apart, or decays, it forms smaller, lighter atoms; releases subatomic particles, which are particles smaller than an atom; and releases energy in the form of heat. This happens slowly and predictably.

What the engineers who designed *Voyager* did was harness this heat. They installed devices that turn some of the heat energy produced by the plutonium into electrical energy. This is the energy that has powered Voyager's communications, computers, and scientific instruments. This tiny nuclear plant has powered all of *Voyager*'s electrical needs, without a break, since it was launched in 1977. Scientists calculate that this tiny power plant should continue to keep *Voyager* running and in contact with Earth until at least 2020. As the plutonium slowly decays, however, the power output is slowly winding down. *Voyager* is running out of fuel.

It was with this hardware and a little more that *Voyager* was outfitted for its journey. *Voyager*'s journey will eventually take it beyond the outermost regions of our solar system and into interstellar space.

Difficulties

Voyager 2 produced some beautiful pictures of Neptune, but it didn't get that many. It made about ten thousand images of Neptune. Ten thousand images may seem like a lot, but considering this was the first close-up look at this world, scientists wanted more pictures to answer many of their questions. *Voyager* made some important measurements, but not as many as scientists would have liked. Scientists like lots of measurements. They can never get enough of them, but taking good measurements and good images far out in space while traveling at high speed is not easy. To appreciate how hard it is to explore a large planet at so great a distance from Earth with a tiny robot spacecraft, it helps to consider some of the difficulties that Voyager encountered.

Difficulty #1: Limited Time

Although *Voyager 2* has often been described as "flying" from one planet to another, its movements have more in common with gliding than flying. It's true that *Voyager* has small rocket engines. These engines work well for minor course corrections, but they are far too weak to propel *Voyager* from planet to planet. Instead, *Voyager* glided from planet to planet. It sped up as it was pulled toward a planet, but this increase in speed was caused by the planet's gravity, not by *Voyager*'s engines. As it moved away from the planet, it slowed down again because of the gravitational pull of the planet it was leaving. *Voyager* rode the gravitational "hills and valleys" of outer space the way a glider rides on air currents. It could control its direction, but it couldn't do much about its speed.

In the enormous empty regions between planets, where the gravitational fields aren't that strong, *Voyager* glided smoothly along at an almost constant speed. There's not much in the big gaps between planets to either speed *Voyager* up or slow it down. In this environment *Voyager* had lots of time to take pictures and measurements, but unfortunately, in interplanetary space there's not much to photograph and there's not much to measure.

The situation was very different whenever *Voyager* approached a planet. As *Voyager 2* came under the gravitational pull of Neptune, the spacecraft began to speed up. It moved as if it were falling down a very deep well. The closer it came to this massive planet, the faster it went. When *Voyager* was near Neptune, there was a lot to photograph and there were many measurements to take but not much time to do either. (After a twelve-year journey, the "near phase" part of the encounter with Neptune lasted less than a week.)

Difficulty #2: Limited Light

Not only was *Voyager* speeding along when it was near Neptune, it was taking pictures in the dark. This means that long exposures were necessary in order for each camera to "build up" an image for transmis-

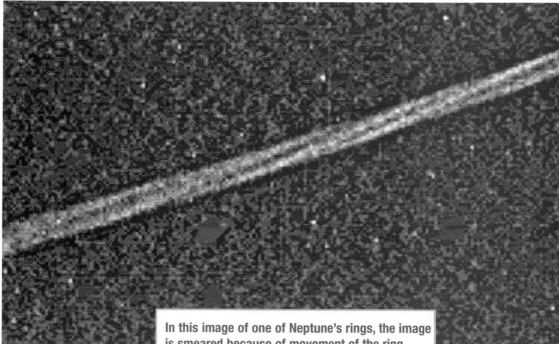

In this image of one of Neptune's rings, the image is smeared because of movement of the ring material while the photograph was being taken.

sion to Earth. When *Voyager 2* visited Jupiter, the light, though dim by Earth standards, was bright enough so that picture-taking was relatively simple. It was almost point-and-shoot. By the time *Voyager* reached Neptune, the light was much dimmer and exposure times were much longer. Keeping the camera focused as *Voyager* careened past Neptune and its moons was not easy. Because of the dim light and high speeds, *Voyager* had to turn its cameras even as it made each single picture in order to keep the image centered in the lens. Failure to do so would have resulted in blurred images. To make matters worse, Neptune itself rotates rapidly—once every sixteen hours.

Difficulty #3: Long-Distance Communications

Voyager was so far from Earth that each radio message took about four hours just to arrive. This means that the simplest round-trip message took about eight hours—four hours to get there and four hours to get back. At the speeds that *Voyager* was traveling in the vicinity of Neptune, eight hours was simply too long a communication lag to make direct control from Earth a practical option. For this reason *Voyager's* simple computers were programmed to control each aspect of the flyby.

The messages from *Voyager* to Earth had one more difficulty: *Voyager* broadcast all of its information across the almost 3 billion miles (5 billion km) that separated us from it with a twenty-three-*watt radio*! By way of comparison, many desk lamps use a sixty-watt bulb, and many coffeemakers and toasters require more than one thousand watts of power to function. Furthermore, after the radio signals had traveled almost halfway across our entire solar system, the signals had spread out so much that they were almost entirely too weak. Scientists expected to have some difficulty receiving *Voyager*'s message, and they did. Fortunately, they had a plan.

To keep *Voyager*'s messages intelligible, NASA scientists slowed down the rate at which *Voyager* transmitted messages back to Earth. For a very weak signal, a slower transmission rate can be "read" with fewer errors. They also programmed *Voyager* to insert additional bits of information into the digital stream that contained the images and measurements of Neptune. This additional information helped them identify problems in reception during reception. It also helped them reconstruct *Voyager*'s initial message when what they received was different than what *Voyager* sent. Such computer codes are called error-correcting codes. NASA has a great deal of expertise in the design of efficient error-correcting codes. That's the good news. The bad news is that these additional error-correcting digits further slowed the rate at which information could be transmitted to Earth. And remember that while *Voyager* can store some information for later transmission, it can't store that much—no more than half a gigabyte.

So there wasn't much time for *Voyager* to collect information. Collecting it took extra time and transmitting it was slow work. *Voyager* couldn't store a lot of information for later transmission, either. So while *Voyager* was a tremendous scientific breakthrough, it couldn't help but leave a lot of work undone and many questions unanswered.

This radio dish antenna at the Goldstone station in California is part of the Deep Space Network that monitored *Voyager*'s signals.

This color composite of Neptune was
created from data recorded by *Voyager 2*.

Chapter 4

What *Voyager* Learned

As *Voyager* careened toward and then past Neptune, it made as many measurements of the chemical composition of Neptune's atmosphere as possible. Some of these measurements confirmed what astronomers had previously measured from Earth. Some of the measurements revealed surprises.

Neptune's atmosphere does contain hydrogen, helium, and methane as well as other *hydrocarbons*. Hydrocarbons are molecules that are made of hydrogen and carbon atoms. Methane is a hydrocarbon. So is acetylene, which is used in welding, and ethane, which is found in natural gas. Neptune's atmosphere also contains ethane and acetylene.

Voyager used its infrared spectrometer, called the Infrared Interferometer Spectrometer and Radiometer, to measure Neptune's temperature. This device analyzes the spectrum of *infrared waves*. Infrared waves travel through space just like light waves. The wavelength of infrared waves is a little longer than the wavelength of red light. We can't see infrared waves. But scientists like to analyze infrared waves as well as light waves, because scientists learn about more than chemistry when they study the infrared spectrum. They also learn about temperature. The infrared spectrometer detects or "sees" heat. This information can be used in determining the composition and the temperature of planetary atmospheres. *Voyager's* infrared measurements came as a surprise. Scientists knew Uranus's temperature, which is -322° Fahrenheit (-197° Celcius). This is, of course, very cold and the natural assumption was that Neptune, which is much further from the Sun that Uranus, would be even colder. Some scientists had even computed how much colder Neptune would be. Remember that Neptune is more than a billion miles further from the Sun than Uranus, so it receives even less solar energy than Uranus. The surprise was that Neptune has essentially the same temperature in its upper atmosphere as Uranus. And Neptune maintains this comparatively warm temperature even though *Voyager* discovered that it radiates away into space *more than twice as much heat* as it receives from the Sun. Somewhere under its big, beautiful, poisonous atmosphere, Neptune has a substantial heat source of its own! The source of Neptune's "heater" is not yet understood.

Another misconception that scientists had prior to *Voyager's* flyby was that Neptune's atmosphere is a very quiet place. They had formed this opinion by comparing Earth and Neptune. On Earth we have a

Taking a Planet's Temperature

Planets don't have just one temperature. On Earth, as you may know from your own experience, it's cooler on the tops of mountains than it is in the valleys below. Generally, here on Earth, the higher you go, the colder it gets. And what's just as important is that on Earth, the further down into the atmosphere you go, the greater the atmospheric pressure. The same is true of Neptune. Neptune's atmosphere extends far below the tops of the clouds that we see in photographs. It's a very deep atmosphere, and the variation in temperature and pressure between the upper reaches of the atmosphere and the lower reaches is much greater than it is here on Earth. So when scientists say they've measured the temperature on Neptune, what does that mean? How do we interpret a single temperature for an entire planet?

First, in order to compare temperatures on different planets, scientists measure temperatures at identical pressures. This takes into account the fact that on every planet, temperatures change as elevation changes. Scientists may not be able to identify elevation, however, because they may not know where the planet's surface is or, for that matter, whether the planet has a surface at all. That's why they give the temperature at a particular pressure instead of a particular elevation. Neptune has an average temperature of -328° F (-200° C) where Neptune's atmospheric pressure is about the same as Earth's atmospheric pressure at sea level. (We call this a pressure of "1 atmosphere.") By contrast, Earth's average temperature at about 1 atmosphere pressure is 55° F (13° C). The temperature of Neptune's lower atmosphere, however, is much hotter than anyplace in Earth's atmosphere. Scientists believe that deep in Neptune's atmosphere, where pressures are very high, the temperature is about 900° F (480° C)!

great variety of weather. Our atmosphere is always in motion. We have powerful hurricanes and tornadoes, monsoons, and blizzards. Enormous warm fronts and cold fronts sweep across the face of our planet. The energy for all of this activity comes from the Sun. Because Neptune receives so little heat from the Sun, scientists assumed that it was, meteorologically speaking, a very peaceful planet.

What *Voyager* observed were some of the fastest winds in the solar system. Wind speeds on Neptune can be more than 1,000 mph (1,600 kph). *Voyager* photographed what was, apparently, an enormous storm system in the southern hemisphere. This system was the size of our planet. They called it the Great Dark Spot, in analogy with the famous Great Red Spot on Jupiter. (The Great Red Spot has been observed in

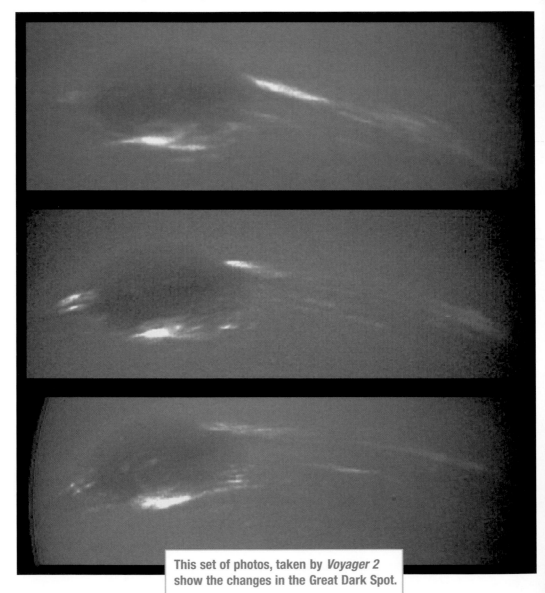

This set of photos, taken by *Voyager 2* show the changes in the Great Dark Spot.

Jupiter's atmosphere ever since the invention of the telescope about four hundred years ago.)

It takes a great deal of energy to cause such massive and sometimes violent motions in Neptune's atmosphere. Presumably the energy comes from deep within Neptune. It can't come from the Sun, because, as we've already mentioned, Neptune doesn't receive much heat from the Sun and it radiates away more heat than it receives. Unfortunately, since scientists can't explain how Neptune is heated from inside, they're so far at a loss to explain the cause of some of the wildest weather in the solar system.

Triton

Voyager found six small, previously unknown moons orbiting Neptune, but one of the most interesting discoveries made by *Voyager* occurred when it turned its instruments toward Triton, Neptune's largest moon. Scientists had long known of Triton. (Remember? They found Triton in 1846 and used their measurements of Triton's movements to estimate Neptune's mass.) But they had no idea that it, like Neptune, was such an active place. First, they discovered that although Triton is somewhat smaller than Earth's Moon, Triton has a thin atmosphere. The main constituent of Triton's atmosphere is nitrogen. Not too many places in the solar system have atmospheres made up mostly of nitrogen. Triton is one. Earth is another. (Earth's atmosphere is almost 80 percent nitrogen.)

And Triton has volcanoes! Unlike Earth's volcanoes, which can eject great rivers of molten rock, Triton's volcanoes eject extremely cold liquids that flow along its frozen terrain before freezing solid. *Voyager* did not observe these volcanoes erupting.

As this *Voyager 2* composite image shows, the surface of
Triton is characterized by a variety of topographical features.

And Triton is very, very cold. *Voyager's* infrared spectrometer determined that it is the coldest place detected so far in the solar system. The surface temperature of Triton was measured with *Voyager's* infrared spectrometer at -391º F (-235º C). This is so cold that much of Triton's atmosphere has frozen solid, solidified, and settled onto the ground.

Triton has geysers, too. *Voyager* observed enormous geysers erupting from the surface that were expelling great plumes of cold, unidentified material. The plumes shot up several miles. They were deflected by winds and eventually settled back onto the surface. *Voyager* also sent back images of great expanses of ice. These were not images of what we know as ice, which is frozen water, but methane ice and nitrogen ice.

Finally, one of *Voyager's* spectrometers detected the faint glow of an aurora in Triton's atmosphere. Many of the planets have auroras. (An aurora that occurs in the northern hemisphere of Earth is called an aurora borealis. In the Southern Hemisphere, it's called an aurora australis.) There are only two moons in the solar system where auroras have been detected. Saturn's moon, Titan, is one. Neptune's moon, Triton, is the other.

Triton is a very strange and wonderful place. There are volcanoes, geysers and auroras. It is so far from the Sun that daytime on Triton would seem like night to us. The nights are even darker. Triton's rough, icy landscape is unimaginably cold. It has a temperature not far above absolute zero, the temperature at which all molecular motion comes to a stop. Triton is as strange a world as any described in science fiction, but it's not science fiction. It's science fact. Triton, like Neptune, is a very active place.

The Rings

As it turned out, the partial rings, the ring arcs, that scientists thought might partially encircle Neptune didn't exist. The "arcs" are bulges within thin rings and are composed of material that's more reflective than the rest of the material in the ring. *Voyager* didn't gather enough data to identify what made these ring bulges more reflective. The existence of the bulges may be explained by the gravitational effects of one of the six moons that *Voyager* discovered. The orbit of this moon lies just inside the ring. The moon's gravity may be causing the ring material to accumulate at certain points along the ring. The points of accumulation are the bulges.

Voyager also gathered a little information on the internal structure of one of the rings by observing a stellar occultation. Officially, the ring was named 1989N1R. It's the ring that contains the bulges. *Voyager* discovered that much of the matter that makes up the ring is concentrated at the inner edge, the edge closest to the planet.

The *Voyager* data were initially interpreted to indicate that Neptune has four rings. Scientists now believe that there are five thin rings encircling the planet.

This image, taken by *Voyager 2*, shows Neptune's ring system. The dark band at the middle comes from a technical problem with the imaging equipment.

Neptune's rings were initially identified with names like 1989N1R and 1989N2R. Later, other, more interesting names were chosen. Of special interest to us are the names given to 1989N1R and 1989N2R. They're now called the Adams and Le Verrier rings, respectively, after the two astronomer-mathematicians who originally calculated Neptune's location from measurements taken on the orbit of Uranus. (Their story is recounted in Chapter 2.)

After the Encounter

The close encounter with Neptune altered *Voyager*'s path. Prior to its Neptune flyby, *Voyager* traveled in what's called the plane of the ecliptic. This is a flat, imaginary surface that contains the Sun and the orbits of all the planets except Pluto. (Pluto's orbit is tilted relative to this plane.) After the flyby, *Voyager* left the plane of the ecliptic on a glide path that takes it south of the ecliptic, further and further from the Sun and deeper and deeper into darkness. It travels along at a steady rate of about 300 million miles (480 million km) each year. Space is so huge, however, that it will be years before *Voyager* leaves the outermost regions of the solar system and tens of thousands of years before it is closer to another star than it is to our Sun.

Voyager is equipped with instruments that allow it to detect the stream of particles that radiates outward from the Sun. The Sun ejects subatomic particles that flow away from the Sun and deep into space. This particle stream is called the *solar wind*. *Voyager* collects data on the solar wind, but the further *Voyager* goes on its journey, the more spread out and weaker the solar wind becomes. Eventually, the solar wind will be so weak that it will simply blend into interstellar space. The Sun's particle stream will no longer be detectable by *Voyager* as a distinct source. At that point, *Voyager* will have officially left our solar system. This final boundary of our solar system, the place where the solar wind blends with the tenuous stream of particles from other stars, is called the *heliopause*. Once *Voyager* passes the heliopause, it will have entered the dark, cold void of interstellar space.

Scientists hope to be able to maintain contact with *Voyager* beyond this point, although no one knows precisely where the heliopause is, so no one knows when *Voyager* will get to it. *Voyager*'s radioactive power source is slowly becoming weaker as the plutonium decays. When *Voyager* left Earth, its tiny nuclear power plant produced about 470 watts of power. Its output, however, diminishes a little with each passing year. It produced about 300 watts in 2002, and it's got nowhere to go but down. *Voyager* is running out of power. NASA has plans to gradually shut off instruments so that *Voyager*'s power requirements don't exceed its dwindling power supply. Their computations indicate that *Voyager 2* should continue to function well enough to enable NASA to maintain radio contact for the first few decades of the twenty-first century. Eventually, however, there won't be enough power for *Voyager* to continue to do useful science. When that happens, *Voyager 2*'s mission will be over.

The *Hubble Space Telescope* in outer space as viewed from the space shuttle

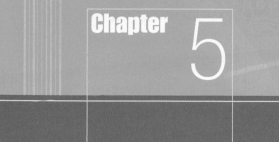

Chapter 5

Neptune After *Voyager*

Only a few months separated *Voyager*'s first inward-bound, faraway picture of Neptune from its last outward-bound, never-to-return picture of Neptune, but it took years for scientists to analyze all of the information that *Voyager* had sent back to Earth. They compared observations. They asked questions: Why are Neptune's winds so strong? Why are there geysers on Triton? They developed theories. They worked hard to understand what *Voyager*'s information meant. Remember that little was known about Neptune prior to *Voyager*'s visit. *Voyager* provided us with our first clear look at the planet, but the encounter was brief. After *Voyager* left, there were no opportunities for it to make follow-up observations.

Although the number of new observations of Neptune didn't increase dramatically for the first few years after *Voyager*, technology was surging forward. The *Hubble Space Telescope*, placed in orbit high above Earth in 1990, is the most famous example. Initially there were problems with the telescope's mirror, but it became fully operational in 1993 and began to send back extraordinary pictures of the planets as well as stars and galaxies.

Ground-based observation technologies were making rapid progress, too. In fact, in recent years they have improved well beyond what anyone would have thought possible when *Voyager* was launched. Within six years of *Voyager*'s flyby, scientists were again making important new discoveries about Neptune's atmosphere. Only this time, they were making their discoveries from almost 3 billion miles (5 billion km) away.

Technology has improved dramatically, but many of the approaches to learning about Neptune remain the same. Astronomers still use optical telescopes to obtain images. They still use spectrographs to obtain information about chemistry and temperature. They even continue to observe occultations to learn about Neptune, its rings, and its moons. Many of the views and measurements obtained with the new, Earth-based instruments rival those obtained by *Voyager*.

Pictures of Neptune taken by the *Hubble Space Telescope* showed that by 1994 the Great Dark Spot, which Voyager had photographed just five years earlier, had disappeared. Unlike Jupiter's Great Red Spot, which astronomers have been observing for centuries, Neptune's Great Dark Spot was relatively short-lived. Observations made in 1995, however, revealed the existence of a new large-scale weather system similar to the Great Dark Spot. This new system developed in Nep-

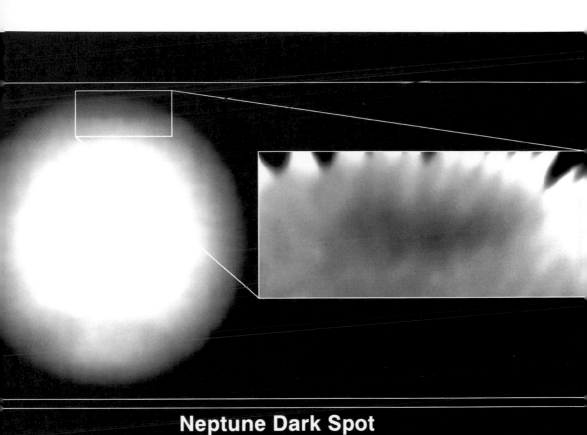

Neptune Dark Spot
Hubble Space Telescope · Wide Field Planetary Camera 2

T ScI OPO · April 19, 1995 · H. Hammel (MIT), NASA

This Hubble view of Neptune revealed a new dark spot.

tune's northern hemisphere, in contrast to the Great Dark Spot, which was located in the southern hemisphere. So Neptune isn't just a place of tremendous winds and enormous storms; it's also a place of rapidly changing weather.

Imaging technology continued to improve, as did the spectrograph on which so much of what we know depends. In 1998 scientists used information obtained from the *Hubble Space Telescope* as well as a spectrograph located at a ground-based observatory in Hawaii to make a sequence of pictures of Neptune. These pictures were then "blended"—with the help of computer imaging technology, merged to create a movie of Neptune's weather patterns. Now we can see the tremendous equatorial winds as well as the distinct weather bands that exist on either side of the equator. We can again see those wispy, white, high-altitude clouds. These clouds form regularly high above the blue clouds that give Neptune so much of its color.

With better technology has come a deeper understanding of Neptune's atmosphere. Scientists now know that Neptune has a methane cycle that is in some ways similar to Earth's water cycle. On Earth, surface water evaporates and the vapor is carried up into the atmosphere, where it condenses and forms clouds and, eventually, returns to the surface as rain or snow. On Neptune, methane vapor is carried aloft in great updrafts where it condenses and freezes and, sometimes, forms high-altitude clouds. Unlike the water on Earth, however, the methane of Neptune's atmosphere sometimes undergoes chemical reactions at higher elevations to form other hydrocarbons. (Ethane, propane, and methane are other examples of hydrocarbons.) These hydrocarbons are destroyed when the clouds are swept down deep into Neptune's atmosphere, where the whole cycle begins again. Of course, this is very interesting information but no one is satisfied with it. It doesn't tell us enough. Scientists would like to learn more about the dynamics of Neptune's atmosphere.

Scientists are now able to combine the results obtained by optical observations and spectrographs to measure variations in the height of

What's Down There?

What's beneath Neptune's enormous cloud cover? More clouds. When scientists have had an opportunity to look through a "break" in the upper cloud deck, they just see deeper into the atmosphere. Unlike Earth, where a break in the clouds gives us a glimpse of the land below, a break in the clouds on Neptune gives us a look at the clouds further down. Neptune's atmosphere is very deep and, with current Earth-based technology, impenetrable. To probe deep inside the planet, scientists rely on measurements of, among other things, Neptune's mass and radius. They rely on mathematics and computer simulations. They also rely on their imaginations for insight into what lies deep within the planet.

What do Neptune's mass and radius tell us about the interior? When scientists know a planet's mass and radius, they can calculate the density of the planet. This is an important piece of the puzzle. Every chemical compound has its own density. Planets are composed of chemical compounds. When scientists know a planet's density, they can draw certain conclusions about the structure and chemical composition of the planet. For example, Earth's average density is a little more than three times that of Neptune's average density. In fact, Neptune is only 1.7 times denser than water. This tells us that the chemical compounds that make up Neptune are much less dense than the materials of which Earth is composed. Knowing the density of Neptune isn't enough by itself for scientists to describe its interior, but it does allow them to eliminate a theory when that theory predicts too great an average density for the planet.

The information presently available about Neptune's interior is not conclusive. Most questions remain unanswered. There is general agreement, though, that Neptune, the planet named after the Roman god of the sea, has a core composed largely, or perhaps entirely, of liquids. A spherical "ocean" roughly the size of Earth seems to lie at the center of Neptune. It's an ocean that may be composed of liquid water, liquid methane, liquid ammonia, and perhaps even some molten rock. Neptune has little, if any, solid surface on which to stand.

Neptune's cloud tops. It is now possible to make crude cloud maps. But while maps are an important first step, scientists are interested in more than facts. Facts are just the beginning. The goal is to develop a physical theory that will explain the motions of Neptune's atmosphere, its tremendous winds, its mighty storms, and its wispy, white clouds.

This may help scientists to better explain weather systems on other planets as well, including our own.

Occultations have continued to play an important role. A stellar occultation was used to reveal the state of Triton's atmosphere. Triton is Neptune's largest moon and one of the few moons in the solar system with its own atmosphere. What these scientists discovered was that Triton's atmosphere had changed since *Voyager's* flyby. In 1989 when *Voyager* made its close approach to Triton, it detected a thin nitrogen atmosphere. Scientists have since used stellar occultations to determine that in the years following *Voyager's* flyby, the atmosphere on Triton has become substantially thicker, or denser. It has also become warmer.

To understand how these scientists measured the density of Triton's atmosphere by observing an occultation, you need to keep in mind that an atmosphere is just a halo of gas. Like the cherry at the center of a cherry cordial, the solid part of Triton is embedded in its halo of gas. During an occultation, the star is occulted by the atmosphere *before* it is occulted by the solid part of Triton. The effect of the atmosphere on the star's light is difficult to observe because the atmosphere is so thin. In fact, in years past, scientists wouldn't have been able to observe the effect of the atmosphere at all. They would have observed only the star's light blink off as the body of Triton passed between us and the star. This time, however, with better technology, they could see much more. This time the technology was so sophisticated that they observed the star's light beginning to dim as the upper regions of Triton's atmosphere occulted the star. It's like a thin cloud passing between you and the Sun. As the Sun's light dims, you learn a little about the thickness of the cloud. By repeatedly and rapidly measuring changes in the star's light, they recorded the rate at which the light grew dimmer as the star was occulted by the denser lower reaches of Triton's atmosphere. This variation in the intensity of the star's light as it shows through different layers of atmosphere was just what scientists needed to know to calculate the density of Triton's atmosphere. Triton's atmosphere had become significantly denser as well as several degrees warmer since *Voyager*'s visit.

Exploring Neptune, The Next Big Thing

It will be a long time before another spacecraft visits Neptune. And although the *Hubble Space Telescope* gives excellent views of Neptune, there's a problem with using *Hubble*: everyone wants to use it. To understand the physics of Neptune's atmosphere, for example, it would help to monitor Neptune regularly, but that's hard to do with *Hubble*. Too many scientists are waiting to use it, and it cannot look everywhere at once.

To understand why so many scientists want to use *Hubble*, it helps to understand what's special about the telescope. It's not that it has the best optical system, because it doesn't. It doesn't have the biggest mirror, either, and in astronomy big mirrors are very important. In fact, *Hubble*'s mirror is small compared, for example, with those at the Keck Observatory in Hawaii. The thing that makes *Hubble* special is that it's positioned high above the atmosphere, and as every astronomer, professional and amateur, knows, our roiling, never-steady atmosphere can ruin the view. Even when the air is crystal-clear, turbulent motions of the atmosphere can blur images in the same sort of way that hot air rising off a highway in summer can make objects further down the road appear to shimmer. Under these conditions, precise measurements can be impossible to obtain.

Keck I (left) and Keck II are located at Mauna Kea observatory in Hawaii. Each telescope uses a mirror with a diameter of 10 meters to focus light.

Adaptive optics is a technology that allows astronomers using ground-based telescopes to nearly cancel out the effects of atmospheric turbulence. The promise of adaptive optics is that every telescope equipped with this technology will have a view that is turbulence-free.

All big telescopes use mirrors to collect and focus light onto special surfaces called *charged coupled devices (CCDs)* which change the image into a form that can be stored and analyzed by a computer. Unfortunately, turbulence in the atmosphere can blur that image. A telescope outfitted with adaptive optics uses a compound mirror to bring the light to a focus. A compound mirror is a mirror that's composed of many smaller mirror segments. It can look sort of like a flattened-out disco ball. Each segment is controlled individually to create a single, large "smart" mirror. We call it a smart mirror because it is programmed to adapt to atmospheric turbulence by changing the shape and tilt of each of its component mirrors. As it rapidly changes shape, it produces an image that is turbulence-free. It "undoes" the effects of atmospheric turbulence and provides astronomers with a clear window into outer space.

How does the mirror "know" how to change its shape? Adaptive optics technology begins with sensors that monitor the conditions of the atmosphere along the line of sight of the telescope. When sensors detect instabilities in the atmosphere—instabilities that cause the image to blur—that information is forwarded to a computer that calculates how these instabilities have affected the image. This information is used to deform the large mirror by tilting and/or bending each of the individual mirror segments. A clearer and more stable image then forms at the focus of the telescope. Adaptive optics technology is

A technician does maintenance on the active optics system of the WIYN telescope at the Kitt Peak Observatory in Arizona.

getting better and better, and it's already quite good. Already, the view from Earth is almost as good as the view from space.

As more telescopes implement this technology, there will be more opportunities for astronomers to obtain frequent, steady, clear images of many hard-to-see objects, Neptune included.

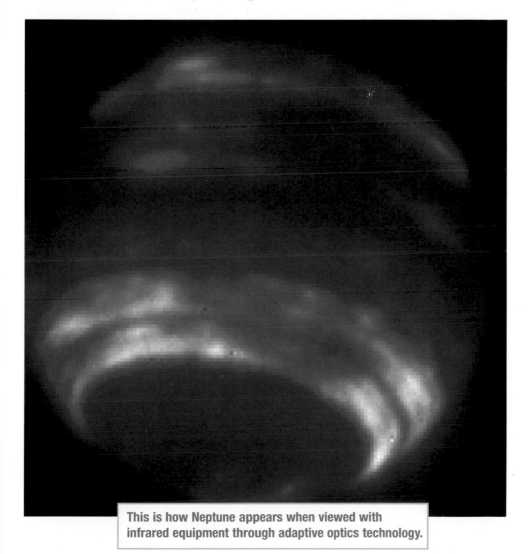

This is how Neptune appears when viewed with infrared equipment through adaptive optics technology.

Future missions, yet to be determined, will provide even more information about Neptune.

Chapter 6

What's Next?

N ASA has no plans to send another spacecraft to Neptune anytime soon, although you can already find a plan for the next Neptune probe on their website. NASA imagines a probe whose design would overcome the difficulties that *Voyager* encountered during its flyby. First, this probe would orbit Neptune so that it could continuously monitor conditions on the planet for a prolonged period of time. Second, the communications system would download information to Earth at much higher speeds than the engineers who designed *Voyager* would have imagined possible. This would allow the transfer of huge amounts of information over very short time periods. And of course, the equipment used to monitor Neptune and Triton would be far more sensitive than that with which Voyager was equipped. As presently envisioned, the probe would plow into the upper reaches of Neptune's atmosphere to slow it down enough to place it in orbit. From its position in orbit, it would inflate very large solar panels so that it could tap into the very weak rays that reach Neptune from our Sun.

For the next several years, further observations of Neptune, its moons, and its rings will depend on Earth-based observatories and on the *Hubble Space Telescope*. But technology is continually improving. The view from here is getting better and better. We can be sure that these observatories will continue to supply new data and that the new data will enable scientists to further improve their understanding about:

• Neptune's weather and how matter and energy are moved about the planet by the winds

• its atmospheric chemistry

• the source of Neptune's warmth

• the physics of Neptune's ring system

• changes in Triton's atmosphere

• the causes and effects of the geological activity taking place on Triton, the coldest known place in the solar system

This, of course, is just a partial list of the unsolved scientific problems associated with Neptune.

But the art of discovery doesn't just consist of refining and fine-tuning old ideas and solving old problems, although, to be sure, this is very important. Discovery also consists of finding new ideas and new problems. We can be certain that Neptune will continue to be a source of challenging, scientifically important problems for the foreseeable future.

Exploring Neptune: A Timeline

1613 — Neptune is observed for the first time in history by Galileo Galilei during observations of Jupiter. Galileo doesn't notice that Neptune is a planet.

1618–1621 — Johannes Kepler publishes his laws of planetary motion.

1687 — Isaac Newton publishes his theory of gravity. The theory of gravity is verified when predictions made with this theory agree with Kepler's laws of planetary motion

1781 — William Herschel discovers Uranus.

1845 — John Couch Adams correctly computes the position of Neptune.

1846 — Urbain Jean Joseph Le Verrier correctly computes the position of Neptune.

Neptune is first recognized as a planet using Le Verrier's calculations.

Triton, Neptune's largest moon, is first observed.

1949	—	Nereid, Neptune's second largest moon, is first observed.
1977	—	*Voyager 2* is launched.
1985	—	Neptune's rings are first detected via stellar occultation.
1989	—	*Voyager* flys by Neptune.
1990	—	The *Hubble Space Telescope* is launched.
1996	—	The *Hubble Space Telescope* makes a movie of Neptune's weather.
1997	—	Changes in Triton's atmosphere are detected by the *Hubble Space Telescope* during stellar occultation.
1999	—	Adaptive optics technology is installed on one of the 33-foot (10-meter) Keck telescopes, the largest telescopes in the world.

Comparing Neptune and Earth

Vital Statistics

	Neptune	Earth
AVERAGE DISTANCE FROM THE SUN	4495.1×10^6 km	149.6×10^6 km
ORBITAL PERIOD	164.79 years	1 year
MASS	102×10^{24} kg	5.97×10^{24} kg
DIAMETER	49,528 km	12,756 km
DENSITY	1,638 kg/m³	5,515 kg/m³
LENGTH OF DAY	16.1 hrs	24 hrs
TEMPERATURE (AT ONE EARTH ATMOSPHERE)	−320º F (−200º C)	55º F (13º C)
MAJOR ATMOSPHERIC CONSTITUENTS	Hydrogen, helium, methane	Nitrogen, oxygen
RINGS	5	0
MOONS	8	1

adaptive optics—a technology used on Earth-based telescopes to counteract the effects of atmospheric turbulence that can produce a view as clear as if the telescope were located in outer space

charged coupled device (CCD)—a device that detects an optical image and changes that image into electrical signals that can be stored by a computer and analyzed

electromagnetic wave—a wave of electric energy, such as light, an infrared wave, or a radio wave

ellipse—a shape often described as a slightly flattened circle. Planetary orbits are almost perfectly elliptical in shape.

heliopause—the boundary between our solar system and interplanetary space, the region where the stream of particles streaming away from the Sun merges with the particles present in interstellar space

hydrocarbons—molecules formed exclusively from carbon and hydrogen atoms

infrared wave—an electromagnetic wave with a wavelength somewhat greater than that of red light

Kepler's laws of planetary motion—discovered by Johannes Kepler; descriptions of (1) the geometry of planetary orbits, (2) the way that planetary speeds change as they move along their orbital paths, and (3) the relationship between the distance of a planet from the Sun and the time it takes the planet to complete one orbit

law of gravity—discovered by Isaac Newton; describes how the force of attraction exerted by two objects on each other is related to the masses of the objects and the distance between them

mass—the amount of material in an object

occultation—a phenomenon that occurs when a planetary body passes between the (Earth-based) observer and a star

perturbation—a small deviation in the elliptical orbit of a planet due to the gravitational pull of its neighbors

solar wind—atomic and subatomic particles that flow outward from our Sun

spectrograph—a device used in conjunction with a telescope to record a spectrum

spectrometer—a device used to measure a spectrum

spectrum—a range of wavelengths for light or other type of wave, where the waves are displayed in order of wavelength. Sunlight passed through a prism forms a colorful spectrum where the colors are ordered by wavelength—longer (red) waves on one end and shorter (blue) waves on the other.

wavelength—the distance, measured along the line of travel, from one peak of a wave to the next. Light travels in waves; we see light of different wavelengths as different colors.

To Find Out More

The news from space changes fast, so it's always a good idea to check the copyright date on books, CD-ROMs, and videotapes to make sure that you are getting up-to-date information. One good place to look for current information from NASA is U.S. government depository libraries. There is at least one and often several in each state.

Books

Bredeson, Carmen. *Neptune*. Connecticut: Franklin Watts, 2002

Hunt, Albert, Garry Hunt, and Patrick Moore. *Atlas of Neptune*. New York: Cambridge University Press, 1994.

Moore, Patrick. *The Planet Neptune: An Historical Survey Before Voyager*. New York: John Wiley and Sons, 1996.

VanCleave, Janice. *Astronomy for Every Kid*. New York: John Wiley and Sons, Inc., 1991.

CD-ROM

The Outer Planets, EOA Scientific Systems, Inc., Nova Scotia, Canada:

Organizations and Online Sites

The Association of Lunar and Planetary Observers (ALPO)

P.O. Box 171302

Memphis, TN 38187-1302

http://lpl.arizona.edu/alpo/

ALPO is one of the oldest associations of amateur observers. It publishes a journal, encourages beginners in observing solar system
objects, and is a good resource for beginning astronomers.

The Astronomy Café

http://www2.ari.net/home/odenwald/café.html

This site answers questions and offers news and articles related to
astronomy and space. It is maintained by NASA scientist Sten
Odenwald.

***Astronomy* Magazine**

http://www.Astronomy.com/

Astronomy is a high-quality, general interest, astronomy magazine.
You'll find the general article about Neptune and lots of information
about astronomy in general. Its website has a number of interesting
features including information about local astronomy clubs.

NASA and *Voyager*

http://vraptor.jpl.nasa.gov/voyager/voyager.html
NASA's website on the *Voyager* mission contains lots of information on the spacecraft itself as well as some of the beautiful pictures that *Voyager* took of Neptune.

NASA and Neptune

http://solarsystem.nasa.gov/features/planets/neptune/neptune.html
NASA's official Neptune website.

NASA Ask a Space Scientist

http://image.gsfc.nasa.gov/poetry/ask/askmag.html#list
Take a look at the Interactive Page, where NASA scientists answer your questions about astronomy, space, and space missions. This site also has access to archives and fact sheets.

NASA Newsroom

http://www.nasa.gov/newsinfo/newsroom.html
This site features NASA's latest press releases, status reports, and fact sheets. It includes a news archive with past reports and a search button for the NASA website. You can even sign up for e-mail versions of all NASA press releases.

The Neptune Orbiter

http://sse.jpl.nasa.gov/site/missions/E/neptune_orbiter.html

This NASA website describes plans for a future Neptune mission.

Neptune's Weather

http://oposite.stsci.edu/pubinfo/mpeg/nept96.mpg

This site offers a movie of Neptune's weather.

The Nine Planets: A Multimedia Tour of the Solar System

http://www.seds.org/billa/tnp/nineplanets.html

This site has excellent material on the planets, including Neptune.
It was created and is maintained by the Students for the Exploration
and Development of Space, University of Arizona.

The Planetary Society

http://www.planetary.org/

65 N. Catalina Avenue
Pasadena, CA 91106-2301

The Planetary Society is a large group of people interested in exploring outer space and in searching for extraterrestrial intelligence.

Sky and Telescope Magazine

http://skyandandtelescope.com/

Sky and Telescope is a high-quality, general interest astronomy magazine. You'll find the occasional article about Neptune as well as a lot
of other information about astronomy. Its website is filled with help-
ful information about many facets of the field of astronomy.

Sky Online

http://windows.ivv.nasa.gov

This is the website for *Sky and Telescope* magazine and other publications of Sky Publishing Corporation. You'll find a good weekly news section on general space and astronomy news. Of special interest are *Sky and Telescope* feature stories adapted especially for online reading. The site also has tips for amateur astronomers as well as a nice selection of links. A list of science museums, planetariums, and astronomy clubs organized by state can help you locate nearby places to visit.

Welcome to the Planets

http://jpl.nasa.gov/planets

This tour of the solar system has lots of pictures and information. The site was created and is maintained by the California Institute of Technology for NASA/Jet Propulsion Laboratory.

Windows to the Universe

http://windows.ivv.nasa.gov

This NASA site, developed by the University of Michigan, includes sections on "Our Planet," "Our Solar System," "Space Missions," and "Kids' Space." Choose from presentation levels of beginner, intermediate, and advanced. To begin exploring, go to the URL and choose "Enter the Site."

Your Local Astronomy Club

http://skyandtelescope.com/

Join your local astronomy club and see Neptune for yourself. Most astronomy clubs have monthly meetings where you can learn all sorts of things, and they'll occasionally set up their telescopes for public viewing. Most serious amateur astronomers have already seen Neptune through their own telescopes. Neptune isn't hard to see if you know where to look, but you can't see it without a telescope. Call ahead of a regularly scheduled public viewing. Explain that you have a special interest in Neptune. If Neptune is visible the night of the viewing, A club member may offer to show it to you. To find an astronomy club in your area consult your local library, local science museum, or the directory maintained by the magazine *Sky and Telescope,* at the web address given above.

Places to Visit

Another exciting way to learn more about science (and maybe a little more about Neptune) is to spend a day at a science museum. There are many good ones in the United States and Canada. Some are so big that it takes days to see everything. Others are smaller but still worth an afternoon of your time. Here's a short list of science museums. Some are famous; others are not. Each is worth a visit.

Center of Science and Technology
333 West Broadway Street
Columbus, OH 43215
www.cosi.org/
A very interesting museum with many creative exhibits. After you've
seen some of the exhibits take a ride on the high-wire unicycle!

Discovery Place
301 North Tryon Street
Charlotte, NC 28202
www.discoveryplace.org/
Wide ranging and creative exhibits.

The Exploratorium
3601 Lyon Street
San Francisco, CA 94123
www.exploratorium.edu/
This is a famous museum with a wide variety of high quality exhibits.

Houston Museum of Natural Science
1 Hermann Loop Drive
Houston, TX 77030
www.hmns.org/
The museum also runs an astronomical observatory that features one
of the largest of all telescopes open to public viewing. The George
Observatory is located in Brazos Bend State Park. There are regularly
scheduled times for public viewing.

The Montshire Museum
1 Montshire Road
Norwich, VT 05055
www.montshire.net/
This is a small, creative, high-quality, hands-on science museum.

The Museum of Science
Science Park
Boston, MA 02114
www.mos.org/
This huge museum takes days to explore fully.

The National Museum of Science and Technology
1867 St. Laurent Blvd.
Ottawa, Ontario K1G 5A3
Canada.
www.science-tech.nmstc.ca/

The National Air and Space Museum
Washington, D.C. 20560-0321
www.nasm.si.edu
This is part of the Smithsonian Institution and it's one of the great museums of its kind in the world. Take time to see the permanent exhibit entitled Looking@Earth.

Odyssium
11211-142 Street
Edmonton, Alberta T5M 4A1
Canada
www.odyssium.com/
Many changes in recent years have made this museum even better
than ever.

Index

Bold numbers indicate illustrations.

John Tabak has a Ph.D. in mathematics and lives in Essex Junction, Vermont, with his beautiful wife, Gail, and their children, Leo and Leela. He owns a battered 8-inch reflecting telescope and is a member of the Vermont Astronomical Society.

Pluto

Uranus

Jupiter

Mars

Mercury

Sun